ITALY

Lombardy

Leonardo Ferrari

Title: Italy, Lombardy

Copyright © Leonardo Ferrari

The author and the publisher have made every effort to ensure that the information contained in this book is complete and reliable. However, they are for illustrative purposes only and therefore the author and the publisher are not liable for the consequences of their use.

First Edition

Table of contents

1. Airports. Access from the airports.

There are three airports in Lombardy:

1.1. Milan Malpensa

It is located about 50 km from Milan. It consists of terminal 1 (main; intercontinental flights, national carriers) and terminal 2 (EasyJet, Alitalia, charter flights).

1.1.1. Malpensa Express

It runs to Milano Centrale (Milan Central; 51 minutes) and Milano Cadorna (37 minutes). The station is located at the airport, on level -1. The train stops at both terminals 1 and 2. Trains run every 30 minutes, in both directions. Tickets can be purchased online or at the ticket office at the station (open 6.30-21.00) and the arrival hall (7.00-21.00). The one-way ticket is 13 euros, the return one is 20 euros. Trains run from 4.27 to 00.20 both from Milano Centrale and Milano Cadorna towards the airport. They leave the airport between 5.26 and 1.30. You will find a detailed timetable here. If someone only needs to move between terminals 1 and 2, the ticket for this train costs 2 euros. However, it is not worth using this option because there is also a free airport bus (every 10 minutes, every 30 minutes at night) between the terminals. The journey takes 8 minutes.

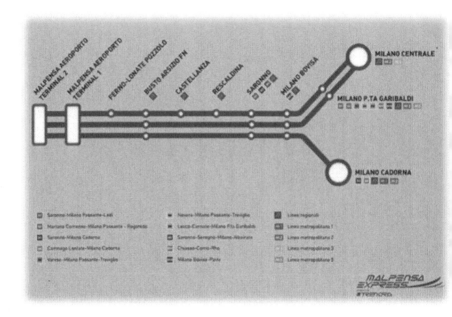

1.1.2. Bus (Malpensa Shuttle)

A ticket to Milano Centrale railway station (possibility to change to the metro or train in other directions) costs 10 euro for a one-way ticket, 16 euro for a return ticket. You'll find this carrier's website <u>here</u>. Tickets can be purchased online or at points of sale, which can be found at both terminals 1 and 2. They are open daily. Buses run every 20 minutes.

1.1.3. Bus (Terravision)

A ticket to Milano Centrale station costs 8 euros (return 14 euros), you can buy it online on this page. The Terravision office in the arrivals hall is open daily from 6.30 am to 8.30 pm. If your flight was delayed and you bought it online for a specific time - you don't have to worry. The ticket is valid all day long. Buses run every 20 minutes. From the airport between 5.05 and 00.10, from the railway station between 3.50 and 9.55 p.m.

1.1.4. Malpensa Bus - Linate (Malpensa Shuttle)

If for some reason you have to move between the two airports there is a direct bus line. Tickets can be purchased online or on board. They can also be purchased at points in the arrival hall in both Terminal 1 and 2 (open 7 days a week). The journey takes between 70-90 minutes. The cost is 13 euros.

1.2. Mediolan Linate

It's practically in Milan itself. National carriers such as Alitalia, Lufthansa, British Airways, Air France are flying in. There are several ways to get from the airport to the center.

1.2.1. Taxi

Stand by the exit from the arrivals hall. The driving time is 15-20 minutes, depending on where our hotel is located.

1.2.2. ATM city bus

The cheapest option. It runs to the Duomo subway station, with intermediate stations. The line is 73 and runs every 10 minutes. The full route from Linate to the Duomo is 28 minutes. Going to the airport the bus has the direction San Felicino (it does not stop at the airport). The first bus from Duomo departs at 5.03, from the airport towards Duomo at 5.30. Cost 1.60 euro.

1.2.3. Bus (Malpensa Shuttle)

It's running to Milano Central. A one-way ticket is 5 euros, a return 9 euros. Tickets can be purchased online or on board. There is also a point of sale in the arrivals hall.

1.2.4. Bus Linate - Malpensa Shuttle

If for some reason you have to move between the two airports there is a direct bus line. Tickets can be purchased online or on board. There is also a point of sale in the arrivals hall. The journey takes between 70-90 minutes. The cost is 13 euros.

1.3. Bergamo (Orio Al Serio)

It is located about 60 km from Milan. The airport is quite well known to low cost tourists due to the fact that it can be reached by cheap airlines such as WizzAir or Ryanair.

1.3.1. Bus (Malpensa Shuttle)

Directly from the airport to Milano Centrale station. The cost is 7 euros one way, 13 euros back.

1.3.2. ATB city bus to Bergamo city centre

The cost is 2.40 euros. It runs every 20 minutes. Tickets can be purchased at the tourist information point in the arrivals hall, it is open from 8.00 a.m. The line is 1A and apart from the station you can go straight to the Old Town and go sightseeing. If not, we can take a train to Milan (or another town).

The Bergamo - Milano Centrale train runs equally every hour. The cost is 5.50 euros, driving time 48 minutes. You can check the schedule on the Trenitalia site here.

1.3.3. Taxi

The distance between the airport and the railway station in Bergamo is only 5 km, so for a larger group of people consider taking a taxi.

1.3.4. Flixbus

It runs from the airport directly to Milan, Verona, Peschiera del Garda, Brescia, for example. Prices in Flixbus are dynamic so it is worth checking if the journey will not come out cheaper and faster than taking the bus to the center of Bergamo and changing trains there.

2. Moving around Lombardy. Io Viaggio ovunque in Lombardy.

2.1 Card options

The card can be purchased for 1 (16.50 euro), 2 (27 euro), 3 (32.50 euro), 7 (43.50 euro) days. If you plan to visit a lot during your stay, the cost of card will be returned to you quickly, especially if you stay for a longer period, e.g. 7 days.

2.2. Where to buy

The card can be purchased at ATM or Trenord ticket machines. It is currently not possible to buy it at the airport in Bergamo. You can buy it only at Bergamo railway station, in one of the numerous newsagents (they usually have a signboard, which indicates that they sell this type of ticket). In other cities it is available at railway and underground stations.

2.3. Children

Children can travel for free until the age of 14 under the care of an adult who has a valid card. The parent should fill out this form before the trip, and keep it with him throughout the whole stay.

2.4 What includes

The card allows unlimited travel in the Lombardy region. The ticket includes:

- All regional trains (not including express and frecciarossa trains). If we travel outside Lombardy we buy (at the ticket office or online on the Trenitalia website) a ticket for the missing section only.

Example: we want to go from Milan to Verona. The zone border ends at Peschiera del Garda. From there to Verona we buy a ticket. In addition, on Io viaggio ovunque in Lombardy we can travel without a 1st class surcharge. This is especially useful in a season when there is a shortage of seats in 2nd class.

- Metro. There are two cities in Lombardy with a metro system: Milan and Brescia.

- Buses. All lines, all over the region. Even 73 in Milan or 1A in Bergamo. Not applicable to private companies, so-called shuttle buses.

- Ferries on Lake Iseo (not valid on Lake Garda or Maggiore).

- Cable railways, so called Funivia and Funicolare, which are included in the ticket price:

  - Margno - Pian delle Betulle, Lecco, funivia
  - Lecco - Malnago - D'Erna Piani, Lecco, funivia
  - Albino - Selvino, Bergamo, funivia

- Campodolcino - Alpe Motta, Sondrio, funivia
- Argegno - Pigra, Como, funivia
- Ponte di Piero - Monteviasco, Varese, funivia
- Bergamo Bass - Alta, Bergamo, funicolare
- Colle Aperto - San Vigilio, Bergamo, funicolare
- Como - Brunate, Como, funicolare

2.5. What to remember

Before first use, you must validate your ticket. If we buy it at the station, it is worth to do it immediately in the punch box (in Italian trains the ticket is validate before entering the train, in the punch box). The date will be reflected on the ticket. The ticket is not read at the subway gates, so you have to show it to the staff at the "booths" at the gates. Very often seeing that you are holding a ticket in your hand they open it without asking. The same applies to cable railways, e.g. in Bergamo, when you show your ticket at the ticket office, you will get another one worth 0.00 euros, which will let you through the gates.

3. Traveling by car

3.1. Parking

The colours of the parking spaces are important in Italy:

- White - free spaces.

- Blue - paid spaces. The payment should be made in the parking meter, and if not, in the nearest tabacheria. We put the ticket behind the car window. The surrounding signs are worth noting. It may indicate that parking is paid, but at certain times, and we will not have to pay when arriving in the evening.

- Yellow - for the disabled.

- Pink - for pregnant women or with small children.

3.2. What to watch out for - Zona Traffico Limitato.

Sometimes it happens that city centres are closed to traffic, only to their inhabitants. So if we see the sign ZTL, be careful! We can earn a ticket. If we know that we will be staying in a hotel, which is located in the very historical center of the city, it is worth to agree in advance with him whether it is possible to park next to his car.

3.3. Highways

3.3.1. Lombardy Highways:

- A1 (Highway of the Sun). Route: Milan, Bologna, Florence, Rome, Naples.

- A4. Route: Turin, Verona, Milan, Venice, Trieste.

- A7 (Highway of Flowers). Route: Milan, Genoa.

- A8 (Lake Highway). Route: Milan, Varese.

- A9. Route: Milan, Como.

- A21. Route: Turin, Alessandria, Brescia.

- A53. Route: Connection between the A7 motorway and Pavia.

3.3.2. Motorway payment

The highways in Lombardy are paid for. At the entrance, a ticket is taken (biglietto). We pay the fee when we get off. Let's choose the right goal depending on whether we want to pay with cash or card (tool booths are well marked). If your card is rejected and you have no other option to pay, the gate will open and a demand for payment within 15 days will be printed. This can be done online here, or alternatively at the next gateway or at the customer service office of a section of motorway (punto blu). It may not be easy so perhaps the easiest option is simply to pay online. If we cannot cope with the gateway, we can also decide to use the red button (ASSISTENZA/HILFE/HELP).

If you would like to check how much the pleasure of using the motorway on a particular section will cost, please do so on this website. Simply enter the appropriate locations in the fields Partenza (z) and Arrivo (do).

3.4. Fueling

3.4.1. Fuel prices in Italy.

In Lombardy, we have to reckon with an average fuel price of 1.50 euros per litre. If we want to refuel cheaply, we can use the Fuel Flash application, available in the Google Play store. It is free and allows you to search for petrol stations with fuel prices on them. Choosing the option of a particular city we can easily see their colors (green - the cheapest, red - the most expensive) on the map.

3.4.2. Types of petrol stations

Petrol stations such as the one in central Europe (large station, with staff) are not popular, we will meet them e.g. near airports. Often this station can only be two distributors standing by the road (without any shop, service). You pour the fuel yourself and pay by card or cash at the distributor. Sometimes you will find the mixed type, where the so-called self-service is possible, but it is also possible to refuel the car by the station staff (piu service). In Italy, this is an extra chargeable option, and the difference can be several cents per liter of fuel!

3.5 Speed limits in Lombardy

- 50 km/h - built-up area

- 90 km/h – non built-up area

- 110 km/h - express roads

- 130 km/h - motorways

3.6 Compulsory equipment when travelling in Italy:

- Warning triangle with approval

- Reflective vests for all passengers

4. Practical information.

4.1 Documents

Italy belong to the Schengen area, which means that people living within Schengen area need only an identity card to cross the Italian border. Of course, you can still travel with your passport instead. Before your holidays, let's make sure that the document you take with on the journey is still valid.

4.2 How to save money during a tour in Lombardy.

Every first Sunday of the month the entrance is free of charge (monuments under the care of the state, i.e. museums, archaeological sites, etc.). If our stay falls on this date, it is worthwhile to arrange our plan in such a way as to benefit from this saving for your wallet.

4.3. Sending a postcard

In Italy, the post office is called Poste Italiane and its logo is typically yellow with blue letters. If we bought a postcard on the stall and do not have a stamp for it, we do not have to look for a post office. We will buy stamps in popular tabacheria shops in Italy. Contrary to its name, we will also buy useful things such as stamps, public transport tickets or pay for parking if there is no parking meter nearby. Let us remember that the stamp in Italian is francobollo, and the stamp for Poland is "francobollo alla Polonia".

4.4. Types of plugs

The voltage in Italy is 220V and 50Hz, so typical for Europe. In the new facilities we will meet with a traditional European nest. However, it may happen that in old buildings we come across an Italian type of socket. These are three holes above each other, with two possible sizes: with larger and smaller spacings between the holes. For the former you will need an adapter, for the latter you will also need a plug with two inputs. If we are in a hotel and it turns out that there are old-type sockets in the room, ask for an adapter at the reception. In general, every good hotel makes such available to guests for free.

4.5 The time zone

Italy is in the GMT +2 zone, the same as in France, Germany, Spain or Poland. This means that when we go on holiday to Lombardy, we have a 6 hour difference between Milan and New York.

4.6. EHIC

The European Health Insurance Card is issued by the branch offices of the Voivodeship National Health Fund at the request of the insured person. This is a message from the NHF:

"European Health Insurance Card (EHIC) - a document which confirms our right to receive medical care in the countries of the European Union and Iceland, Liechtenstein, Norway or Switzerland on the same basis as persons insured in a given country, in facilities operating within the general health care system, in urgent cases".

The NHF urgently calls urgent actions on its website as:

- "They are medically necessary, taking into account the nature of these benefits and the duration of the stay,

- They were granted to avoid the patient being forced to return to the territory of the country of affiliation in order to receive the necessary treatment."

Making a card is free of charge so it is worth taking care of the formalities before our journey and taking it with us. It is also worth considering buying additional travel insurance privately, for the time of the holiday.

4.7. Smoking

Smoking in restaurants is completely banned in Italy. This includes restaurants, pizzerias, bars, pubs, cafés and discos. So we can only smoke a cigarette in the open air.

5. What is Lombardy famous for?

5.1. Aperitivo

Milan is seen as the cradle of aperitivo, i.e. the time of day (usually 18.00-22.00), during which for the price of one drink (usually 8-9 euros) we have a buffet available, which we can use at will. It depends on the class of the restaurant and its reputation whether we will be offered simple snacks or several types of warm dishes. Aperitivo has spread and now we can meet them all over Lombardy. But it is Milan that is most strongly identified with him. Italians like to visit several places with their friends that evening. In the capital city of Lombardy, the Navigla district, the old canal district, is particularly popular. It is worthwhile to stroll along them and find a place whose climate will suit us.

5.2 The capital of finance

Lombardy is the richest and most developed region of Italy. It is the headquarters of the Italian stock exchange as well as numerous banks and corporations. It is called the financial and economic capital of Italy. Italians come here from the south. Per capita income in Lombardy is 142% of the EU average. Lombardy accounts for a quarter of Italy's GDP, although about one sixth of the country's population lives there.

5.3 The world's fashion capital

Milan hosts numerous trade fairs and fashion weeks. We can buy clothes there from the best designers and tailors. Exclusive boutiques and clothing stores are popular. Many of the most expensive ones are located in the famous Vittorio Emanuele II Gallery.

5.4. Alfa Romeo Museum

It is located in Arese, about 18 kilometres from the centre of Milan. The easiest way to get there is by subway to Rho-Fiera station (line 1). Then we change to bus line 561, which stops in front of the museum door. The museum is open from 10-18, closed on Tuesdays. The ticket price is 12 euros.

5.5. Monza track

Known to car lovers. The Formula 1 competition takes place there. Admission is free from Monday to Friday. On weekends the ticket price depends on the event that takes place on the track. The track is very close to Milan (about 20 km from the city centre). You can get there by train, which runs on average every 12 minutes, or by bus 204 from Corso Milano to Vedano.

5.6. Winter sports

Lombardy is famous for modern winter resorts such as Livigno, Tonale, Bormio and Madesimo. If you're a ski lover, you won't be disappointed with the tracks in Lombardy.

6. Food. What should we taste?

Appetisers:

- Cheese: Mascarpone, Grana Padano, Gorgonzola, Taleggio, Quartirolo Lombardo, Provolone Valpadano, Rosa Camuna.

- Cold cuts: Bresaola della Valtellina, Cotechino alla Bergamasca, Coppa Mantovana, Salame Brianza,

Salame Cremona, Salame Milano or Salame Mantovano.

Main dishes:
- Risotto alla Milanese (also called Risotto allo Zafferano). Risotto is popular throughout northern Italy, but it is a speciality of Milan. Prepared on broth and beef marrow, seasoned with saffron, to which it owes its colour.

- Trippa alla milanese. Guts prepared with beans, tomato pulp, carrots and celery.

- Cassoeula. Winter single-potted dish prepared from various kinds of pork (e.g. bacon, legs, ribs) with cabbage. Formerly, a dish of the poor similar to that popular in this region, although it comes from Veneto, polenta.

- Ravioli (Tortelli) di Zucca. Ravioli with pumpkin filling. Coming from Mantua, it is said that it was first served at that court in 1549! Traditionally eaten for Christmas, now you can meet them on the daily menu. The filling is prepared from the persistent varieties of pumpkin and Amaretti cookies.

Desserts:
- Panettone. A Christmas cake from Milan. The classic version includes raisins and candied lemon and orange peel. Nowadays, there are numerous flavor variations, e.g. with pistachio cream or lemon cream.

- Colomba. Yeast-shaped Easter cake. Decorated with almonds. Like panettone stuffed with raisins and peel.

- Filascetta. A kind of pretzel, resembling bagel, with the addition of cheese, red onion and a bit of sugar. Especially popular around Lake Como.

- Polenta e osei. A cake from Bergamo, currently one of the most important symbols of the city. Yellow ball of marzipan filled with hazelnut cream and chocolate butter.

Alcohol:

- Campari. Bitter (bitter liqueur) from Milan, whose history dates back to 1860. It consists of herbs, spices, bitter orange peel. He has 25% alcohol. Campari has even had its own museum.

- Franciacort wine. This is a sparkling wine from the province of Brescia. Produced from grapes grown in the hills between the shores of Lake Iseo and the town of Brescia.

- Amaro Ramazzotti. Herbal liqueur (30%) soothing indigestion, whose history dates back to 1815. It consists of 33 herbs and spices.

Others:
- Mostard. A mixture of candied fruit and mustard. The most spicy one is the one from Cremona (multifruit), then successively from Voghera, Milan and Mantua (apples only). It works well as a seasoning for meat, cold cuts, cheese, especially in autumn and winter.

7. Tour plan

It is addressed to people who are going to this wonderful region for the first time. The proposal I made is a minimum option. This means that every place in the tour plan is beautiful and you can spend more time there. Everyone has an individual pace of travel and interest, so the plan can be treated as an inspiration that can be freely modified. Let's also bear in mind that in summer, when the day is long, we have much more time to visit than in winter. At the end you will find the attachments, i.e. a map of communication in Lombardy and a diagram of the Milan metro. All prices are valid as of the date of writing the book. The author is not responsible for changes in ticket prices and opening hours of selected attractions or the functioning of means of communication, as these are things beyond his control.

Day I. Departure. Bergamo

If we travel by low-cost airlines and get to Orio al Serio airport, we only have a few hours to go, it will be a great point of the program. We have a chance to stretch out after the flight. If we decided on a hotel in Bergamo we can leave our luggage there. If our accommodation is located in another city, it is worth using a luggage box. It is located opposite the Bergamo railway station (you should cross the street, the boxes are right next to McDonald's). There are two types of cabinets, smaller for 3 euros, bigger for 4 euros. Two suitcases will enter the larger ones easily. Best to have some coins behind you. The boxes are self-service and it will be difficult to change large denominations of banknotes (the option of buying some sweet baked goods in the bakery next door and changing the money remains in the end).

The new district of the city is called Bergamo Bassa, the old town surrounded by walls is called Bergamo Alta. There are two cable railways (funicolare) in Bergamo, which are free for holders of the Io Viaggio Ovunque in Lombardy, about which I wrote earlier. The first one we get from

Citta Bassa to Citta Alta (the alternative is bus number 1, which also goes to the Old Town). The second cable railway is the one that enters the hill of San Viglio (where the ruins of the castle of the same name are located). The entrance offers us unique views of the city and its surroundings, especially at sunset.

Attractions:

- Santa Maria Maggiore, Romanesque church, 9-12.30; 14.30-18. At its back Tempietto di Santa Croce X century.

- Capella Colleoni, 1476, admission free, 9.30-12.30; 14-18.30. Its façade is a true architectural gem, together with the adjacent baptistery.

- Duomo. Open Monday to Friday 7.30-12.30; 15.00-18.30. On Saturdays 7.00-19.00.

- Piazza Vecchia - the main square of the city with a fountain of lions, Torre Civica (12th century) with a beautiful sundial, Palazzo della Ragione (Palace of Wisdom) in Venetian style. It leaves Via Colleoni's main street.

- Fort Rocca - paid (5 euro), free garden by the walls. 14th century.

- Conviento di San Francesco Monastery. You will find there the Bergamo History Museum and the Museum of Photography, among others.

- Castello Di San Viglio - the ruins of a castle which offers a great panoramic view of the city. The highest vantage point can be reached through the passageway in the castle tower. Free entrance, open 24 hours a day.

- Orto Botanico Lorenzo Rota, free entrance, 10.00-20.00 - a small botanical garden that is worth visiting to rest for a while on a bench among the greenery. There is also a tap with drinking water, which you can replenish your water supply.

Day II. Milan

- **Cathedral (Duomo).** The ticket is 3 euros (the entrance to the cathedral itself, more expensive tickets are also available, e.g. entrance to the roof of the cathedral). Open 8-19, you can buy the ticket online. It's worth starting the day with a tour of the Duomo while it's still empty around. There are no queues even in June at 8:00. Both self-service ticket offices and a ticket office are available for visitors. Around 9.00 a.m. the first organised tours start to appear on the Cathedral Square. Inside we will see, among others, the Battistero Paleocristiano (4th century, the place where St. Ambrose was baptized by St. Augustine in 387), the crucifix with a nail from the Cross of Christ and the sculpture of St. Bartholomew.

Note: Remember that the outfit is checked and we will not be admitted to the cathedral unless we dress properly. Already in the queue to the ticket offices someone from security may approach us and point out that if we don't have something to impose on ourselves or disguise it makes no sense to buy a ticket. Therefore, if you are visiting the cathedral in the summer and you are planning to visit it, it is worth packing some lightweight sweater in your backpack to respect this beautiful place. Duomo subway station.

- **Gallery Vittorio Emanuele II** - here you will find boutiques of the most expensive brands as well as a 7-star hotel. It's right next to the Duomo. It's mandatory to look at the floor. There are coats of arms of various cities of united Italy. Apparently, turning on your heel, three times around your own axis, on the bull's testicles of Turin brings luck! The lane is open 24 hours a day.

- **La Scala** (the world's most famous opera). We will reach it by passing from the Cathedral Square through the Vittorio Emanuel Gallery. It's pretty inconspicuous on the outside, so you can easily overlook it. The interiors are more impressive, so it is worthwhile to come here for one of the performances or visit the small museum, which is located in the building.

- **Pinacotheca Brera** - for painting lovers. We can find here paintings of such artists as: Bramante, Rafael, Tintoretto, Caravaggio, Canaletto. Open Tuesday to Sunday, 8.30am to 7.15pm and the standard ticket costs 15 euros. The library, which is one of the largest public libraries in Italy, is also worth a look. The opening of both the Pinacotheque and the library is thanks to Maria Theresa Habsburg.

- **Brera Botanical Gardens.** Admission is free, but to find a passage you have to enter the building (there is no charge for staying on the premises), in the middle there is an internal courtyard. One of the passages under the cloisters leads to the garden. Unfortunately, the google maps are going crazy there and they are driving us to the wrong place. The garden is not big, but there are no tourists there, so it is a good place to relax among the greenery. There are also free toilets in the building, which can be taken into account when planning a visit to Milan.

- **Via Fiori Chiari, Via Fiori Oscuri -** as we continue our walk from Brera towards the castle we will pass the artistic part of the city. These streets are one of the most charming in Milan.

- **Castello Sforzesco** - The castle has three courtyards. Inside we can see a wonderful art collection, the Egyptian Museum, the Museum of Prehistory, or the Museum of Musical Instruments. Behind the castle is Parco Scampione (Milan's largest park), with an impressive triumphal arch. Free entry every first and third Thursday of the month from 14.00. The ticket price is 5 euros and the museums are open from 9.00 am to 5.30 pm. Closed on Mondays and holidays such as 25.12, 1.01 and 1.05. Cairoli Castello Metro Station (but also Lanza, Moscova).

- **Church of St Maurice** (Chiesa di San Maurizio al Monastero Maggiore). After leaving the castle grounds, it is really worth seeing this hidden treasure of Milan. Overlooked by guides and excursions, it offers us beautiful frescoes depicting biblical scenes and those from the lives of saints. They are well preserved, admission is free, there are no crowds. They're really memorable.

- **The Last Supper.** I think everyone has heard of this famous work by Leonardo da Vinci. If you want to see them during your visit to Milan, you must book your tickets online as soon as possible. They spread like warm buns, even a few months before the deadline. When there are no appointments and you are very keen to see the Last Supper, a chance to show up at the ticket office at 8 a.m., then the tickets are sold "reclaimed". The masterpiece can be seen in the refectory of Santa Maria delle Grazie Church. It is located very close to the castle and the church of St. Maurice mentioned above. The cost of the ticket is 15 euros.

- **Stazione Centale** - the largest railway station in Italy. When visiting Lombardy by train, you will have the opportunity to admire it every time. You enter the platforms through the gates, where the control checks if you have a ticket. The platforms are numbered consecutively. On the general schedule, the platform numbers are given, and at each platform, in addition, an electronic board displays the information about where the given squad is leaving. So the station, although large, is rather functional and it is not difficult to find "our" train. In the underground, the station is connected to the underground station.

- **Bosco Verticale** (Vertical Forest) and Gae Aulenti Square. Porta Nuova or Garibaldi subway station. Famous green, self-sufficient skyscrapers, winners of many awards. Over 900 trees grow on them. Next to it is a modern square with a futuristic fountain and modern buildings around. Prestigious location where many career-makers would like to work. There is also the highest skyscraper in Italy (Torre Unicredit, 231 meters).

- **Tre Torri - City Life.** New city district. Its name comes from three towers, three famous architects (in everyday language straight tower, curved tower, twisted tower). Built on a new station, a new subway line. They are adjacent to modern residential buildings and an architecturally interesting shopping mall. It is worth it if you are a fan of modern architecture. Tre Torri subway station.

- **Monumental Cemetery** (Cimitero Monumentale di Milano). Called the open-air art gallery. A place where you can calm down. Monumentale subway station.

- **Basilica di San't Eustorgio.** This is where we can see the sarcophagus with the remains of the Three Kings. The first building was built here as early as in the 4th century, later rebuilt many times. For many years it was one of the stops of pilgrims travelling to Rome. It is very close to the Navigla channels.

- **Navigli** - a district of two canals (Naviglio Pavese and Grande), and Happy Hours (previously mentioned Aperitivo). We can get there by subway (Porta Genova station) or tram (numbers 2 and 9). Milan's favourite place for evening outings and relaxation after work.

If someone has little greenery and still has some strength he can go to the Giardini della Villa Reale (with the former residence of Napoleon) and the **Giardini Pubblici**, large city parks.

Day III. Lake Maggiore

Stresa and the Borromean Islands

The easiest way to get to the Stresa is by train. From Milano Central Station, the regional train will reach the Stresa in about an hour. If you are a holder of the Io Viaggio Ovunque in Lombardy (IVOL) card, you will travel to Arona for free. From Arona to Stresa you should buy a ticket for the missing Arona-Stresa episode (cost 2.80 Euros) from Arona to Stresa in the Trenitalia application or at the ticket office in Milan station. This is due to the fact that Stresa is formally part of Piedmont. Because of the fact that the journey from Lombardy is so fast and easy, and the town is practically just outside the border of these regions, I decided to include this point in this sightseeing programme.

The route of the train runs along the shore of the lake, the views are extremely picturesque. We can admire, among other things, the castle of Rocca di Angera drawing on the opposite bank.

Stresa is a relatively small town with only 5000 inhabitants. It is a beautiful resort town situated on Lake Maggiore. At the Grand Hotel des Iles

Borromees created and placed his novel "A Farewell to Arms" Ernest Hemingway. Along the shore of the lake we can walk on an elegant promenade (lungolago), enjoying the beautiful views. We will be accompanied by well-kept flower beds. You can also have a relaxing splash in the lake. If you want a drink overlooking the lake, you can relax in the Sky Bar at the Hotel La Palma. The bar is located on the roof, on the 7th floor.

Another attraction is the cable car to the top of **Mottarone**. In 20 minutes you will be at 1492 m. The cost of a return trip in summer is 20 euros. If you are interested, you can find more details on the official website of the cable car. On top, in addition to enjoying the magnificent panorama, you can visit the Alpine Garden (cost 4 euros).

However, what attracts to the Stresa are the **Borromean Islands.** When you get from the train station to the waterfront, facing the lake, go right. There will be smaller and larger booths offering transport to the islands. It's not worth buying in the first place. Prices may vary significantly depending on the option selected. You can buy a ticket back and forth to only one island, or to all of them. It all depends on your preferences and the time you have. Remember not to lose it because it'll be checked every time you get on the ship. We used the public carrier Navigazione Laghi, which operates traditional ferries. You can choose private carriers who have smaller and larger boats. Crossing to all the islands costs about 16.90 euros.

The name of the Borromean Islands is derived from the Borromeo family. The islands have been in their possession from the 14th century to the present day. The Borromeans still have the exclusive right to fish in the waters of Lake

Maggiore. The archipelago consists of five small islands, three of which interest us:

Isola Bella (Beautiful Island)

Most of the island is occupied by a fenced palace area and the adjacent garden. The Count Charles III began the construction of this beautiful Baroque foundation for his wife Isabella. This is where the name of the island comes from (the diminutive name Isabella to Bella). The whole thing was supposed to resemble the shape of a ship. The tour starts with a walk through the palace chambers.

There is only one direction of the tour so it is impossible to get lost or miss something. From each of the chambers there is a wonderful view of the lake, adjacent islands and the coastline delirious on the horizon. The equipment of each of the chambers is very rich and impressive. At the lowest level there are rooms imitating caves and shells, decorated with marine motifs. We go directly from there to the gardens.

It is worth entering every alley and alleyway to not miss such attractions as bamboo "forest" or a small greenhouse with orchids. The permanent residents are white peacocks walking proudly through the area.

The entrance ticket to the palace costs 17 euros. I recommend a combined option with the entrance to Isola Madre. The price is 24 euros. All information about other ticketing options can be found here.

There are also some charming narrow streets on the island where we can buy local souvenirs, eat or drink good espresso while waiting for the next ferry.

Isola dei Pescatori (Fishermen's Island)

The island with the highest density of population from the Borromean Islands. There is a fishing village and several restaurants that specialize in fish dishes. Many tourists stay on Fishermen's Island for a quick lunch to taste local delicacies.

Isola Madre (Mother Island)

The largest of the Borromean Islands archipelago and at the same time the furthest from the Stresa. The whole area of it is ticketed, so there is no point in going for it if you are not going to buy admission tickets. The first palace foundation was built right here. The palace is older, but architecturally much simpler than that of Isola Bella. That doesn't mean it's less interesting. In its interior you can admire, among other things, an exhibition of puppets. A chamber with illusionist, floral frescoes also makes an impression.

The island is one big botanical garden. A valuable specimen is the largest Kashmir cypress in Europe (over 200 years old), growing in front of the palace. It is now fixed with ropes. In 2006, during a massive storm, it was pulled out of the ground together with its roots. Fortunately, he was saved and planted again. The old and beautiful collection of azaleas, rhododendrons and camellias, which literally flowed into the lake together with the mass of land, also suffered. Now the botanical garden has returned to its shine. It is worth visiting it especially in spring and early summer, when everything is stunningly green. During our visit in June, there were huge blue hydrangeas in full bloom.

Day IV. Lake Como

Lecco - Varenna - Lenno (Villa del Balbianello) - Como

If you would like to experience the beauty of nature while in Milan and at the same time not waste energy on long and difficult journeys, Lecco will be a great choice for you. You can get here from Milan (Milano Centrale) in 39 minutes. What we're interested in here is the cable railway to the viewpoint, which you can take for free with our Io Viaggio Ovunque in Lombardy.

Piani d'Erna. Getting off at Lecco station we are interested in Via Montello bus stop. This is not a stop, which is located right at the exit from the station, you should go through the station square gently to the left. We're looking for a bus line 5, direction Piani d'Erna. You'll find the bus timetable here. This is his final stop. The route is 30 stops, which the bus goes on schedule in 27 minutes. However, it is worthwhile to have a time buffer.

The bus passes the steep serpentines under the lower station of the cable railway in the last section of the route. The route is extremely picturesque.

It should be mentioned that the bus makes a loop at the station. So it may happen that when you get on the Via Montello, you take the route immediately towards the cable railway. It may also happen that you will take the route by the promenade, go around the tourist centre, go back to the railway station and only then you will go towards the railway. The drivers will tell you if they're going to cable car in both cases. It's not worth panicking and getting off such a bus, because you'll probably get on it anyway when you get back to the station stop. When you get to your destination it is worth taking a picture of the return timetable, but if someone forgets it, the timetable is also at the exit/entry to the upper station. For motorists, there is a car park at the lower station of the railway. The cable railway works every day. Climbing fans may be interested in the fact that ferrata leads to the top.

The wagon is glazed on all sides so that the entrance to the top provides amazing views. On the spot only a few hundred metres separates us from the view point, which is breathtaking. A panorama of the mountains, the city of Lecco at its feet and Lake Como. The picturesque alpine green meadows lead us to it. If we have time and strength, we can go on a hike on one of the trails, e.g. Sentiero Natura. If not, we can sit on a bench and soak up the atmosphere of the Bergamen Alps. Access to the viewing point does not require special preparation or condition. The place is even suitable for a trip with children and a picnic.

From Lecco we're taking the train further to **Varenna**. The route is picturesque, it stretches along the lake. After a short journey it is worthwhile to stroll through this picturesque town. An interesting attraction for people in good shape can be the conquest of Veccio Castle. It offers beautiful views of the surrounding area (10-19, 4 euros). The oldest church in town and on the whole lake is Oratorio di San Giovani (10th century). A popular point of interest is Villa Monastiro. There are quite a few fabulously located villas on Lake Como, so if you have a limited budget and time it is worth choosing the ones that interest you most. In Varena we can take a ferry to other beautiful towns. We can buy an all-day ticket or decide to buy individual episodes individually.

Bellagio. Located on a characteristic promontory, it offers us the opportunity to visit places such as Villa Giulia, Giardini di Villa Melzi or Villa Serbeloni. Gardens very often climb on terraces and the town is considered to be trendy. So we'll meet here with luxury, closed-circuit hotels. It's worth admiring them when we arrive at the port. In this itinerary I suggest to see the Bellagio only from the side of the lake, because it is on the route of the next attraction we want to visit.

Villa Carlotta. Tremezzo. The next stop on our ferry. Although we're sailing further, it's a great point if we stay over Como longer, or any of the previous attractions on this day didn't seem interesting to us. The villa is located in a beautiful botanical garden. A ticket costs 12 euros. The facility is open daily from 10-17.

Lenno: Villa del Balbianello. We've arrived at our destination. From the ferry port we can choose two routes. Shorter, asphalt (also nice) and longer, climbing uphill and then descending from it (practically no tourists). If you have time, it's worth pick one for one way and the other to come back. The ticket to the gardens is 10 euros, the ticket to visit the interior of the villa is another 10 euros. It is definitely worth buying a ticket to the gardens, which are captivating. They are well taken care of, amazingly situated. Their value were appreciated by James Bond himself, who appeared here in one of the scenes of Casino Royale. The villa is open from 10 am to 6 pm.

Note: closed on Mondays and Wednesdays.

On that day we can return to Varenna by ferry and from there take a train to Milan. The second option is to catch a ferry and return to Milan by train through Como.

The city of **Como** is located about 50 km from Milan, on Lake Como. This lake is shaped like an inverted Y, and Como lies at the beginning of its left branch. Lenno, where we were in this morning lies at the beginning of his right leg. We can easily get here from Milan in 40 minutes by train. The station is called Como S. Giovanni. Also here we can take advantage of the free entrance (thanks to our card) to the viewpoint, more precisely from the Como-Brunate cable railway.

You can reach the cable railway by walking past the harbour and walking along the lake, the lower station of the cable car is right next to it. The distance from the station (or from the port if we arrive by boat) is small and undemanding, and the views are beautiful. The train runs from 6.00 a.m. to 10.30 p.m. and in summer and on Saturdays until midnight.

Most people at the level of the upper station end their trip. They admire the views, drink coffee and go back to the Como centre. However, they lose the opportunity to walk in the stunning surrounding of nature. A beautiful hiking route leads to the Volta lighthouse, Il Faro Voltiano. Some people who move on decide to use the services of private persons who offer entry to the viewing point by off-road vehicle. It's not worth it. The cars follow an ordinary asphalt route, pedestrians follow a beautiful marked trail among the greenery and silence.

There are free public toilets in front of the lighthouse itself, but it is literally a hole in the ground. So do not expect comfortable conditions if you travel with children. The lighthouse stands on the viewing terrace, which offers a fairly wide panorama of both the city and Lake Como. A ticket to the inside of the Volta lighthouse costs 2 euros for an adult and 1 euros for a child under 18 years old. Many people give up on entering the lighthouse. They think it offers nothing more than the viewing terrace it stands on. It's a mistake. By crossing these additional steps at the end of our hike we also cross the tree line. This opens up a whole new perspective on the rest of Lake Como. It is heading towards the Bellagio where merging with its second ramification. The view is staggering. The azure of water meandering between overgrown to the top, green mountains.

You can find the current opening hours of the lighthouse <u>here</u>.

Day V. Lake Garda

Desenzano del Garda - Sirmione

I suggest you take the train to **Desenzano del Garda.** From Milan it will take us 1 hour 20 minutes. In the village itself there is a castle and the Roman Villa Crocifisso. The town is charming, but for many people it is only a place where they can change to a bus (preferably from the train station, free of charge for IVOL card holders) or to a ship (faster and easier way, but remember that in this case it is paid for, because the ferries on our card are free only on Lake Iseo).

Our target is **Sirmione.** In the season it is quite crowded. Located on a long promontory extending deep into Lake Garda. The landform and the local hot springs have long been appreciated. We can visit the ancient Grotte di Catullo. These are the ruins of the Roman villa of the poet Katullus. Next to the ruins there is a very interesting beach called Jamaica. There's a beach bar where you can buy a drink in the season. If we want to feel a little bit of comfort, we can use the offer of paid thermal swimming pools Aquaria Thermal Spa. Sirmione's attention is certainly drawn to Scaligerich Castle. From his tower there is a wonderful view of the surroundings. It's really worth paying for your entrance ticket and enjoying the panorama. The singer Maria Callas had her home in town. The best way to explore the city is to get lost in its streets, admire its charming buildings and discover its alleys.

Day VI. Lake Iseo

Sulzano - Monte Isola

Both from Milan and Bergamo to Lake Iseo will require a train change in Brescia. It is worth going to **Sulzano** from where you can take the ferry to Monte Isola (remember that the ferry is free for Io Viaggio Ovunque in Lombardy). You can check the current ferry schedule <u>here</u>.

Monte Isola is the largest island in Italian lakes. One of the most interesting places on the island are the chapel of Madonna della Seriola, which offers a beautiful view of the lake and Castello Oldofredi (Rocca Martinengo). Currently it is not possible to visit the castle because it has been converted into a hotel, but you can decide to have lunch in the hotel restaurant. You can also rent a bike and go around the island or go on one of the hiking trails. Remember, the island is quite steep. The mountain in the heart of the island is about 600 m. If you have enough time, you can consider visiting one of the other places on Lake Iseo, such as Iseo, Sarnico or Lovere by ferry. Of all the big lakes in Lombardy, it's the quietest and calmest on Iseo. Therefore, if you are looking for less commercialized directions, Lake Iseo may be a great choice for you.

Day VII. Return to the country

Alternatives. Of course, you can't see all the attractions of Lombardy during ond week. Therefore, here are some additional inspirations if your stay is longer, or if you want to modify one of the days I have given you.

Ponte nel Cielo (Campo Tartano) - the highest hanging bridge in Europe (the so-called Tibetan bridge; height 140 m, length 234 m). It offers a panoramic view of the valley, the mountains, the dam, the passes and then Lake Como. Open 7 days a week, 9.30 am - 4.30 pm. Ticket price is 5 euros. The easiest way to get to Morbegno is by train and then by bus to Campo Tartano. Check the bus schedule here.

Brescia is the second largest city in the region. It even has its own subway. Worth seeing: Piazza della Loggia (Venetian-style square), Palazzo della Loggia (the square of the same name currently houses the Town Hall), Torre dell' Orologio, Porta Bruciata (Burnt Gate), Cathedral (third highest in Italy) and Rotonda (12th century) in Piazza Paolo VI, the Monastery of San Salvatore-Santa Giulia (the building now houses the City Museum) Capitolino (73 AC Roman temple) and the other ruins of the Roman city of Brixia (theatre, rows of columns perhaps belonging to the forum). We'll get here by train (Brescia station) without any problem.

Pavia - this is a city with a long and interesting history. Charles the Great himself crowned himself king here in 774. It is worth seeing: a very interesting bridge (Ponte Coperto), Brolleto (town hall), the cathedral (Leonardo da Vinci and Bramante took part in its construction), the Basilica of San Michele Maggiore (its most precious treasure is a silver cross from the 7th century), Castello Visconteo (a castle from the 14th century, where we can now visit the City Museum). We'll get here by train (Pavia station) without any problem.

Certosa di Pavia, a monastery located about 8 km from Pavia, has been the seat of the Carthusians, Cistercians and Carmelites in its history. It is now in the hands of the Cistercians again. It is a beautiful example of late Gothic architecture. The impressive marble facade of the church attracts attention. We'll get here by train (Certosa di Pavia station) without any problem.

Cremona - the city is famous for its famous Stradivarius violin. To this day, Cremona produces instruments using a method developed several hundred years ago. There is even a museum dedicated to them, the Museo Stradivariano. Worth seeing: Piazza del Comune with the highest bell tower in Italy (112 m) and the church of St. Peter over the Po (XVI century) decorated with interesting frescoes. We'll get here by train (Cremona station) without any problem.

Mantua. Beautifully located city (the star of the series available on the Netflix platform, Il Processo). Worth seeing are: the Basilica of San't Andrea standing at Mantegna Square (built to house relics, two ampoules with the blood of Christ), the Rotonda di San Lorenzo (modelled on the Basilica of the Holy Sepulchre in Jerusalem), the Piazza delle Erbe, the Palazzo della Ragione (with an impressive tower and sundial), the

Palazzo Ducale (more than 500 chambers!) and St Anselm's Cathedral (patron of the city). We'll get here by train (Mantova station) without any problem.

Monza track - Formula 1 competition takes place there. Admission is free from Monday to Friday. On weekends the ticket price depends on the event that takes place on the track. The track is very close to Milan (about 20 km from the city centre). You can get there by train, which runs on average every 12 minutes, or by bus 204 from Corso Milano to Vedano.

Alfa Romeo Museum - Located in Arese, about 18 kilometres from the centre of Milan. The easiest way to get there is by subway to Rho-Fiera station (line 1). Then we change to bus line 561, which stops in front of the museum door. The museum is open from 10-18, closed on Tuesdays. The ticket price is 12 euros.